Original title:
Snowbound Nights

Author: Eliora Lumiste
ISBN HARDBACK: 978-9916-79-474-6
ISBN PAPERBACK: 978-9916-79-475-3
ISBN EBOOK: 978-9916-79-476-0

Veiled in Glistening White

Snowflakes dance in whispered air,
Veils of white, beyond compare.
Softly shrouded, world so fair,
Nature's beauty, beyond all care.

Branches bow with gentle weight,
Silence speaks of winter's fate.
Footprints mark the frozen state,
In this wonder, I await.

Nightfall's Frosty Caress

Stars awaken, skies turn deep,
Winter's breath, a secret keep.
Moonlight shimmers, shadows creep,
In this chill, the world does sleep.

Frost has painted every street,
Blanket soft beneath my feet.
Whispered breezes, cold and sweet,
Nature's lullaby, a treat.

Shimmering Blankets

Fields of white, a sparkling sea,
Every flake, a mystery.
Underneath, the earth shall be,
Sleeping softly, wild and free.

Mountains wrapped in silver sheen,
Winter's magic, pure and clean.
Dreams take flight, like birds unseen,
In this realm, my heart can glean.

Hibernal Whispers

Whispers echo through the night,
Nature's song, a soft, sweet flight.
Snowy mutes the world in white,
Winter's grace, a pure delight.

Creatures nest in cozy dens,
Quiet moments, soft amens.
In the stillness, life begins,
Hibernal tales, where warmth transcends.

Flickers of Warmth

In shadows deep, a candle glows,
Soft whispers dance where the fire flows.
Each spark ignites a heart's true call,
Binding the night, uniting us all.

Through winter's chill, we gather near,
In moments soft, we feel no fear.
With every flicker, hope takes flight,
Filling our souls with pure delight.

A Lantern's Glow on Frozen Paths

A lantern sways in the frosty air,
Casting its light with gentle care.
Each step we take, the path unveiled,
Guided by warmth, we shan't be derailed.

Beneath the moon, the snowflakes gleam,
Mirroring dreams that softly teem.
In frozen silence, our fears dissolve,
As the lantern's glow begins to evolve.

Whirling Snowflakes

Whirling softly, they dance and play,
In a world of white, they find their way.
A gentle touch upon my cheek,
Nature's whispers, serene and meek.

Every flake a story untold,
Embodies secrets, timeless and bold.
As they settle, a blanket forms,
Transforming life through winter storms.

The Whispering Woods at Night

Beneath the starlit, velvet sky,
The woods awake, and shadows sigh.
Whispers of trees in soft refrain,
In this serene, enchanted domain.

Curled up tight in nature's embrace,
Time stands still in this special place.
With every rustle, the night unfolds,
A tale of magic, nature holds.

Frosty Footprints

In the early morning light,
Snowflakes dance with pure delight.
Footprints mark the silent ground,
Nature whispers all around.

Each step leaves a story bare,
Crystalline chill fills the air.
The world is hushed, a gentle thrill,
As winter's breath, so soft, is still.

Branches laden, softly bend,
While the icy winds descend.
A trail of dreams in frosty hue,
Guides the heart to mornings new.

Night's White Hush

Underneath the starry skies,
A blanket soft where silence lies.
Snowflakes drift and softly fall,
In the night, they don't make a call.

Moonlight glimmers on the snow,
Whispers of the night do flow.
The world asleep, wrapped in peace,
In winter's arms, all worries cease.

Frosty air, a breath so light,
Holding close the magic night.
Each moment feels like a dream,
Where echoes of time softly gleam.

A Still Night's Cover

The evening fades, a silent sigh,
As shadows stretch and softly lie.
A cover of white, pure and bright,
Drapes the world in soothing light.

Crickets hush their nightly song,
While the stars above shine strong.
Each flake that lands is poetry,
Kissed by cold eternity.

Peace enfolds, a gentle shroud,
In this moment, still and proud.
Winter wraps us, heart anew,
In a world that's fresh and true.

Echoing Winter's Breath

In the twilight, shadows grow,
Echoes of the wind will blow.
A breath of winter sweeps the land,
Crafting visions, bold and grand.

Crisp and cold, the air does bite,
As stars awaken, pale and bright.
All around, the silence sings,
Touching hearts like gentle wings.

Nature's brush paints scenes of white,
In the depth of this serene night.
Each echo carries tales untold,
Whispers of a world so bold.

Frosted Moonlight

A silver hue on icy ground,
Whispers of night all around.
Stars twinkle in the crystal air,
Nature's breath, a silent prayer.

Softly shining, the moon glows bright,
Casting shadows, dancing light.
The world wrapped in a dreamy veil,
Every heartbeat tells a tale.

Footsteps crunch on frosty trails,
Underneath the moon, it prevails.
Echoes linger, sweet and clear,
In this moment, time stands near.

Trees adorned with sparkling frost,
In this beauty, none are lost.
Every branch, a work of art,
Touch the magic, feel its heart.

Snowflakes drift like whispered dreams,
In the stillness, nothing seems.
Wrapped in peace, the night unfolds,
Frosted stories left untold.

Enchanted by the Cold

Whispers of winter in the air,
Enchantment lies everywhere.
Frozen lakes, a glassy sheen,
Nature's palette, pure and clean.

Snowflakes spiral, dance and fall,
Covering earth like a gentle shawl.
The silence deep, a soothing balm,
In the cold, we find our calm.

Pine trees hold their coats of white,
Guardians of the tranquil night.
In this realm of frosted dreams,
Hope glimmers under moonlit beams.

Footprints leading to the vast,
Moments cherished, memories passed.
Hand in hand, we brave the freeze,
Wrapped in warmth, hearts find ease.

Softly cradled in the glow,
Of a world lost in the snow.
Here, we pause and watch the stars,
Under the spell of winter's charm.

Tales in the Wintry Dark

In shadows deep, the stories blend,
Whispers of night, where dreams ascend.
Under the gaze of the weary moon,
Silence hums a gentle tune.

Winds carry tales from far away,
Of distant lands where children play.
Laughter echoes, faint but clear,
In the heart of winter, they draw near.

Branches creak under icy weight,
Each sound, a passage to relate.
Stars sprinkle stories across the sky,
While frost weaves patterns, oh so sly.

Lost in thought by fireside glow,
Tales of warmth amidst the snow.
Time unwinds in chilly air,
Magic lives in every prayer.

As winter deepens, nights grow long,
In each shadow, there's a song.
A tapestry of dark and light,
We weave our dreams in wintry night.

Emptiness Wrapped in White

An endless stretch of snowy plains,
Where silence reigns and memory wanes.
A canvas blank, with whispers nigh,
As fleeting shadows drift and sigh.

Clouds gather low, a heavy shroud,
Emptiness lingers, stark and loud.
In the quiet, echoes trace,
Ghosts of laughter, lost in space.

Frost-kissed breezes brush the trees,
Murmurs carried on the freeze.
A heart once full now feels so bare,
Yet finds comfort in the air.

Every flake, a fleeting thought,
In this stillness, wisdom's sought.
Wrapped in layers, thick as night,
Finding solace in the white.

But in the void, a spark ignites,
A flicker glowing in the nights.
For emptiness, though vast and wide,
Holds a beauty deep inside.

Lullabies for Winter's Heart

The snowflakes dance in the night,
Whispers of dreams soft and light.
Wrapped in warmth, the world sighs,
As winter breathes beneath the skies.

Moonbeams scatter on frozen streams,
Creating a quilt of silver dreams.
Silent lullabies fill the air,
Cradling the earth in gentle care.

Each flake tells tales of the past,
Moments fleeting, yet they last.
A melody drifts through the trees,
Carried softly on the breeze.

Sleep now, dear world, close your eyes,
Forget the troubles, the lows, the highs.
In this calm, let your spirit soar,
For winter's heart will always roar.

Embrace the peace in the cold,
Within the silence, warmth unfolds.
As echoes linger, time finds rest,
In winter's lullaby, we are blessed.

Frosty Footprints

In the early morning light,
Frosty footprints, pure and white.
They tell stories, where I've been,
In a world so crisp and clean.

Each step crunches on the ground,
Nature's silence all around.
Fields of white stretch wide and far,
Guiding me like a silver star.

As I wander through the frost,
In this moment, I feel lost.
Yet each path leads me to peace,
Where the winter's charm won't cease.

The trees wear coats of icy lace,
Nature's beauty, a pure embrace.
Each breath forms a cloud in the air,
Winter whispers, soft and rare.

Frosty footprints lead the way,
In a world that fades to gray.
But in this chill, my heart's alive,
For in winter's art, dreams thrive.

A Canvas of Silence

Blanketed earth, soft and white,
A canvas of silence, pure delight.
Crisp and clear, the air hangs still,
Nature's hush, a gentle thrill.

Clouds drift lazily overhead,
Painting the sky a deep shade of red.
In the quiet, echoes remain,
Whispers of snow, a soft refrain.

Footsteps crunch, breaking the calm,
Each sound like a soothing balm.
In this world of winter's grace,
Time slows down, a warm embrace.

Stars shimmer in the frost-lit sky,
Glistening dreams that pass us by.
In this silence, hearts find space,
To breathe, to feel, to find our place.

A canvas waiting, vast and wide,
Where hopes and dreams can softly glide.
In winter's silence, we are free,
Painting moments, you and me.

Echoes Beneath the Ice

Beneath the surface, stories lie,
Whispers trapped where shadows ply.
Echoes dance in chilly streams,
Quiet secrets, forgotten dreams.

Ice reflects the world above,
Captured moments, lost in love.
Each crackle sings of years gone by,
A winter's tale beneath the sky.

The moonlight shines on frozen lakes,
Rippling softly, the stillness quakes.
Researching depths with fragile grace,
Searching for life's hidden face.

Echoes linger, soft and clear,
Revealing what we hold dear.
In a world draped in frosty light,
Remembering warmth in the night.

Beneath the ice, the heart does beat,
A rhythm strong, a pulse discreet.
In frozen realms where time stands still,
We find the strength to dream and feel.

Shivering Shadows

In the twilight's grip, they sway,
Whispering secrets, lost and gray.
Dancing lightly, fading fast,
Echoes of the day that passed.

Moonlight drapes them, soft and pale,
Casting stories in the veil.
Flickering forms in silent night,
Shivering shadows hold their plight.

A soft breeze stirs, they quiver low,
Murmurs of tales we'll never know.
Each flicker tells of hopes once bright,
In the shadow's enveloping light.

They weave through dreams, both dark and deep,
Harboring sorrows, secrets to keep.
In every corner, they seem to play,
In the haunting silence, they quietly stay.

Yet in their dance, a beauty found,
In the stillness, a mystic sound.
Shivering forms, lost in time,
Speak of longing in rhythmic rhyme.

A Canopy of Stars Above

Under a blanket of twinkling lights,
The universe whispers, enchanting sights.
Each star a story, a wish on the rise,
Painting our dreams across vast skies.

Glimmers of hope in the navy's embrace,
Guiding lost souls to a warm place.
They shimmer gently, a celestial sea,
In the cool night, they set hearts free.

A cosmic tapestry woven with grace,
Tales of old across time and space.
Cradled beneath the Milky Way's light,
We find our courage in the night's height.

The echoes of laughter float on the air,
Carried by stardust, free from despair.
As constellations dance in silent glee,
We revel in wonder, just you and me.

In the vastness, we find home sweet,
With every heartbeat, the universe beats.
A canopy of stars wraps us tight,
In the arms of the universe, we take flight.

In the Embrace of Glacial Dreams

In icy realms where silence reigns,
Time is still, a soothing chain.
Gentle whispers of frost and snow,
In glacial dreams, our spirits flow.

Crystalline visions twinkle bright,
Illuminating the depth of night.
They lead us through a world so pure,
A tranquil place, where hearts endure.

Echoes of nature, serene and clear,
In frozen beauty, we lose our fear.
Each breath a cloud, each step a dance,
In the embrace of dreams, we take a chance.

With jagged peaks and valleys deep,
In silence profound, our thoughts we keep.
The chill wraps close, but souls stay warm,
In glacial whispers, we find our calm.

Awakening wonders beneath the stars,
Connecting our hearts with ancient scars.
In dreams entwined, we are aglow,
In the embrace of ice, we learn to flow.

The Stillness of Sparkling Earth

In the quietude of morning's light,
The world begins to wake from night.
Each blade of grass, a diamond's gleam,
Reflecting nature's perfect dream.

The dew-kissed petals, soft and rare,
Whisper secrets to the air.
In stillness, life holds its breath tight,
Suspended in beauty, pure delight.

Time slows down in this sacred place,
Every heartbeat, a gentle grace.
Sparkling earth beneath our feet,
In each moment, we feel complete.

Nature's song in silence sings,
A melody of simple things.
In the hush of dawn, hope is reborn,
Embraced by light, a new day's dawn.

Let us linger in this tranquil sphere,
Where every whisper, we hold dear.
The stillness of earth, a precious worth,
In its embrace, we find our mirth.

Glacial Echoes of Tomorrow

Whispers of ice in the silent air,
Footprints of dreams, once laid with care.
Time drips slowly, like melting stone,
In the quiet, we find we're not alone.

Fragments of light dance on the frost,
Memories linger, never lost.
Nature's breath in a shimmering hue,
Echoes remind of the path we knew.

With each shard that glistens bright,
Hope arises in the still of night.
Through chilling winds, a spark ignites,
Guiding us to future sights.

Frozen tales held in the breeze,
Speak of tomorrows and unseen keys.
The glacier groans, yet flows with grace,
Unraveling time in this sacred space.

Night's Embrace in White

Stars slip softly through the veil,
Wrapped in silence, we set sail.
Moonlight drapes like a gentle shawl,
Night's embrace whispers to all.

Snowflakes tumble, a silent cheer,
Each one unique, yet draws us near.
In the quiet, shadows twine,
Hearts entwined like roots of vine.

Whispers of dreams in crisp air rise,
Shimmering light in hidden skies.
With every heartbeat, our spirits soar,
Guided by love forevermore.

The world sleeps in a tranquil hue,
Canvas painted in white and blue.
Underneath the clock ticks slow,
In night's embrace, our worries go.

A Solitary Hearth Amidst the Frost

By the window, flames flicker bright,
A cozy glow in the biting night.
Outside the world is wrapped in white,
Inside, a heart beats warm and light.

Amidst the frost, a haven stands,
Crafted with love by gentle hands.
The scent of wood, a soothing balm,
In this sanctuary, all is calm.

Stories linger in the air,
Dreams shared softly without a care.
With laughter echoing in the corners,
The hearth becomes a place for mourners.

Every crackle sings of days gone by,
Comfort wrapped like a lullaby.
In solitude, joy lights the gloom,
Transforming the quiet into a room.

Through iced windows, stars peek in,
Bidding welcome, inviting kin.
In every ember, memories glow,
A solitary hearth, love's warm flow.

The Lull Before the Thaw

The world holds still, in a breath of peace,
Nature waits for winter's lease.
Silence blankets the woods and streams,
Preparing for the sun's sweet beams.

Frosted trees wear crowns of white,
Stars above twinkle with delight.
Each moment stretched in quiet grace,
Time slows down in this sacred space.

Beneath the chill, life stirs anew,
Whispers of green in the morning dew.
Guardians of spring, they rest and dream,
In the hush, all things gleam.

Gentle breezes tease the air,
Hints of warmth that soon will share.
This lull, a promise wrapped in mist,
Of brighter days that none can resist.

As sunlight kisses the frozen ground,
The lull will break with a joyful sound.
Hope awakens from winter's grasp,
Embracing life in a tender clasp.

Solitude in the Frosted Silence

In the quiet, blankets white,
Frosted branches kiss the night.
Whispers dance upon the air,
Solitude, a gentle dare.

Footsteps faint on crystal trails,
Echo softly where night prevails.
Stars above like diamonds gleam,
In the silence, lost in dream.

The moon hangs low, a silver eye,
Watching secrets, passing by.
In this calm, the heart will find,
Peaceful thoughts in winter's kind.

Snowflakes drift like whispered words,
Stories told by silent birds.
Embrace the chill, be not alone,
In the frost, a warmth is sown.

Nature sleeps in soft repose,
Wrapped in dreams, where stillness grows.
Frosted silence, deep and wide,
Holds the world where we abide.

A Night Beneath the Northern Lights

Underneath the dancing skies,
Colors swirl and gently rise.
Emerald greens and fiery red,
Magic woven overhead.

Silhouetted trees stand tall,
Nature's splendor, a beckoning call.
In the hush, the heart takes flight,
Beneath the glow of starry night.

Whispers linger on the breeze,
Carried soft through ancient trees.
In this realm where time stands still,
Moments captured, night distills.

With every hue, a story told,
Of journeys lost and dreams of old.
Awakening the soul's delight,
A night beneath the northern light.

Hearts entwined with nature's pulse,
Under skies that gently convulse.
In the glow, all fears take flight,
Underneath the starry light.

The Art of Winter Whisperings

Listen close to winter's call,
Whispered secrets, soft as fall.
Each breath mingles with the chill,
Painting echoes, memories still.

Frosted windows, paintings pure,
Nature's art, a soft demure.
In the quiet, dreams ignite,
With the whispers of the night.

Footsteps crunch on icy ground,
In the stillness, peace is found.
Voices carried on the breeze,
Woven through the sleeping trees.

The world adorned in shades of white,
Guides the heart to take to flight.
In winter's hands, we find our way,
Through whispered dreams of night and day.

With every flake, a tale unfolds,
Of warmth and love the season holds.
In winter's grasp, the heart will sing,
The art of life, a gentle spring.

Chilling Tales of Solitude

In the hush, where shadows creep,
Whispers of the night, we keep.
Chilling tales the silence weaves,
Woven softly through the leaves.

Hearth fires burn with gentle light,
Flickering like dreams of night.
Outside, the world is clad in white,
Inside, we find our hearts take flight.

Footsteps echo, shadows play,
In the dark, they slip away.
Tales of sorrow, tales of grace,
In solitude, we find our place.

Winter nights hold secrets deep,
In the stillness, souls can weep.
Yet from tears, new stories bloom,
In the silence, banish gloom.

Every breath a tale to share,
Chilling moments fill the air.
In this quiet, life's refrain,
Tales of solitude remain.

Elysian Chill

In the hush of twilight's breath,
Softly falls the silent dew,
Whispers of a frozen dance,
Underneath the sky so blue.

Gentle winds caress the trees,
As stars begin to gleam and glow,
Nature's beauty, pure and still,
A tranquil world, in peace we flow.

Moonlight drapes the hills in white,
A cloak of calm, a dreamer's sigh,
Footprints vanish, lost in time,
Where the heart learns how to fly.

Echoes of the night unfold,
Through the mist, we lose our way,
Caught in the magic of the chill,
Surrendering to shadows' play.

In Elysium's quiet space,
We find solace, we find grace,
As the chill wraps round us tight,
Filling souls with pure delight.

The Quiet of Frosted Evenings

The sun dips low, the sky grows dark,
A chill creeps in, a soft remark,
Frost paints windows with its lace,
In the quiet, we find our place.

Shadows stretch across the ground,
Where whispers of the night abound,
Stars twinkle in the crisp night air,
Breath visible, hearts laid bare.

Every sound seems to retreat,
Wrapped in warmth, we find our seat,
With mugs of cocoa, laughter shared,
In this moment, love declared.

Outside, the world wears silver glow,
While inside, fires crackle slow,
The frosted evening beckons near,
Inviting memories to appear.

As minutes pass, the chill deepens,
Yet hearts are warm, spirit strengthens,
In the quiet of these nights,
We find joy in simple sights.

Icy Reveries

Dreams unfold in winter's grasp,
Where icy breath begins to clasp,
Each flake a whisper, pure and bright,
Painting stories in the night.

Through frosted panes of crystal clear,
Past visions dance, they draw us near,
In silence, hearts begin to soar,
Chasing echoes, seeking more.

Frosty trails of gleaming light,
Guiding souls through starry night,
Where wishes hang like silver threads,
And hope is woven 'neath our beds.

With every breath of winter's air,
We find the magic hidden there,
In icy realms, we learn to dream,
And let our spirits gently beam.

In the stillness, time suspends,
With icy reveries, we make amends,
To nature's call, we softly sigh,
In winter's hold, we learn to fly.

Glistening Dreams

In the dawn, the world aglow,
Snowflakes twirl, a dance, a show,
Each glinting crystal, pure delight,
Whispers of dreams that take to flight.

Through valleys deep and mountaintops,
Where sunlight kisses, never stops,
Glistening paths of endless white,
Lead us on till day turns night.

A canvas vast, untouched, serene,
As nature stitches seams of green,
With threads of gold and silver beams,
We wander through our glistening dreams.

The air is crisp, inviting us,
To journey forth, to wander thus,
With every step, a heartbeat sighed,
In harmony with winter's tide.

So let us chase these dreams alight,
In every shadow, every height,
For in the chill, we come alive,
In glistening dreams, we learn to thrive.

Crystalline Nocturne

Underneath the starlit sky,
Whispers dance with moonlit sighs.
Every shimmer holds a dream,
In the night's enchanting beam.

Glistening on the winter's breath,
Silence drapes the world in death.
Frosted branches, diamond-like,
Nature's beauty, pure and strike.

A symphony of colors sigh,
In the stillness, questions fly.
Each note of night, a story told,
In the crystalline, bright and bold.

Time stands still in this embrace,
Every heartbeat keeps the pace.
Wrapped in warmth of chilly air,
Lost in love, we linger there.

Underneath the starlit veil,
Hearts entwined, we weave a tale.
In the shadows, dreams ignite,
Crystalline within the night.

The Tapestry of Winter

Snowflakes fall in pure delight,
Weaving patterns, soft and light.
Each flake a story to unfold,
In the chill, a warmth we hold.

Silent trees, adorned in white,
Guard our secrets, hidden tight.
Branches bow beneath the load,
Nature's quilt, a soft abode.

Fires crackle, whispers shared,
In the glow, we feel prepared.
Hot cocoa warms our waiting hands,
As outside, the beautiful expands.

Footprints trace our journey here,
In the snow, we leave our cheer.
Memories stitched in frost and air,
A tapestry beyond compare.

Winter nights, serene and deep,
Under stars, our dreams we keep.
In this season's gentle fold,
The tapestry of life, retold.

Frost's Gentle Touch

Morning light on silver gleam,
Frosted whispers softly dream.
Nature's breath, a cool caress,
In its touch, a quiet bless.

Petals shimmer, edges bright,
Every garden dressed in white.
Delicate, the world does sway,
In the glow of winter's play.

Birdsong flutters through the air,
Every note, a sweet affair.
In the chill, we find our peace,
Frost's embrace, a soft release.

Underneath the icy veil,
Stories drift with every trail.
Nature whispers in our ears,
Frost's gentle touch calms our fears.

As the sunlight starts to break,
All the world begins to wake.
In the warmth, we shed the frost,
In its beauty, never lost.

Shadows in the Snow

Footsteps echo through the night,
Shadows dance in pale moonlight.
Every hush, a story told,
In the snow, a realm of gold.

Branches cradle secrets deep,
In their arms, the world does sleep.
Winter whispers, soft and low,
Hidden tales in shadows glow.

Frosted air, a breath of time,
In the silence, hearts align.
Nature weaves a tapestry,
Of whispers bound in mystery.

Stars reflect on drifts of white,
In their gleam, we find our light.
As the world begins to sigh,
Shadows move, and dreams comply.

Beneath the frost, life waits awake,
In the cold, we make no mistake.
Every shadow, every light,
Crafts our love in winter's night.

Winter's Veil

Snowflakes fall soft and white,
Blanketing the world in light.
Trees stand tall, bare and proud,
Wrapped in silence, still and loud.

Footprints crunch on paths unseen,
Nature sleeps in slumber keen.
The air is crisp, a breath of frost,
In winter's grasp, nothing's lost.

Fires crackle, warmth we seek,
Stories shared, hearts will speak.
Hot cocoa in steaming mugs,
Cocooned in love, the world shrugs.

Stars twinkle in the velvet night,
Moon hangs low, a silver light.
Whispers dance on winter's breeze,
In this beauty, our souls find ease.

With every breath, the season glows,
In the stillness, magic flows.
Winter's veil, a tranquil shroud,
Binds us close, a dream endowed.

Whispering Frost

Morning breaks with icy breath,
Nature's hush, a silent depth.
Frosty patterns lace the ground,
In every corner, beauty found.

Bare branches creak in chilly air,
Whispers float without a care.
The brook is still, a glassy face,
Reflecting dreams in frozen grace.

The sun peeks through, a golden grin,
Chasing shadows, battles win.
Winter hues in shades of blue,
Paint a canvas fresh and new.

A snowman stands with scarf in place,
Joyful laughter, a fleeting trace.
Children play, snowflakes chase,
Moments captured, a warm embrace.

As twilight casts its gentle hand,
The frost weaves magic across the land.
Stars awaken, twinkling bright,
In whispering frost, the world ignites.

Silent Moonlit Dreams

Under the moon's soft silver glow,
Whispers of night in ebb and flow.
Dreams take flight on tender beams,
Wrapped in peace, silent dreams.

Shadows dance beneath the trees,
Swirling gently in the breeze.
Stars align in cosmic schemes,
Guiding hearts in moonlit dreams.

Time stands still, a breathless pause,
Nature's beauty, a perfect cause.
In quiet corners, love redeems,
Found in the hush of moonlit dreams.

A lullaby of night unfolds,
Stories whispered, secrets told.
With every sigh, the world redeems,
Woven softly in moonlit dreams.

As dawn approaches, light will gleam,
Yet carry forth those night-time themes.
Forever etched, our sweetest themes,
Nestled deep in silent dreams.

Chill of the Evening

As daylight wanes into the night,
The chill descends, the air feels light.
Stars emerge in velvet skies,
A tapestry of twinkling eyes.

The hearth glows warm, inviting near,
Whispers shared, voices clear.
Wrapped in blankets, hearts align,
Together, we sip the finest wine.

The wind it howls, a ghostly sound,
Echoes through the sleeping ground.
With every breeze, stories weave,
In shadows cast, our hearts believe.

Outside the world, a frosty scene,
Nature's beauty wrapped in sheen.
Through frosted panes, we find our dreams,
In the chill, our laughter beams.

As stars begin their nightly dance,
We hold each other in a trance.
In moments shared, love's permit,
The chill of evening, we gladly fit.

Beneath the Snowy Canopy

Whispers of silence drift so low,
A blanket of white, soft as a glow.
Branches laden, heavy with dreams,
Nature rests in frosted beams.

Footprints vanish in the hush,
As shadows dance in a gentle rush.
The world, serene, in purest sight,
Beneath the canopy, cloaked in night.

Every flake a story spun,
Underneath the icy sun.
Crystals spark in winter's grace,
Hidden treasures find their place.

A hush envelops all around,
In this enchanted, silent ground.
The stars peer down from skies above,
In this snowy veil, we find love.

Breath of winter, sharp and clear,
Embracing joys, dispelling fear.
Beneath the branches, dreams take flight,
In the heart of the winter night.

Frost-Laden Dreams

In the morning light, ice does gleam,
As dawn awakens a frosty dream.
Fields of silver, crisp and bright,
Nature savors the sheer delight.

Each breath a cloud in the cold air,
Whispers soften, a moment rare.
Frosted petals, delicate and small,
Nature's beauty enchants us all.

Quiet moments, the world stands still,
Liquid crystals form on the hill.
In the chill, our hearts find peace,
Frost-laden dreams never cease.

Through the window, a picturesque scene,
Muffled laughter, filled with sheen.
Memory lingers, warm and sweet,
In the frost, our souls meet.

A cradle of dreams beneath the frost,
In winter's embrace, we know no loss.
As stars emerge in twilight's gleam,
We linger in our frosted dream.

Nightfall in Frozen Fields

The sun dips low, shadows stretch wide,
In frozen fields where secrets hide.
Nightfall whispers in shivering tones,
As chilly winds caress the stones.

Moonlight bathes the world in silver,
As ice crystals start to quiver.
Stars awaken, twinkling bright,
Guiding hearts through the tranquil night.

Every breath hangs in the air,
Touched by winter's gentle care.
In the stillness, solace grows,
Where time slows down, and wonder flows.

Darkness cloaks the earth in peace,
As icy fingers bring release.
Footprints fade on paths unknown,
In frozen fields, we roam alone.

Beneath the stars, our spirits soar,
With every heartbeat, we explore.
Nightfall's magic forever yields,
In the charm of frozen fields.

Stargazing Through the Ice

Beneath the frost, the earth is still,
A canvas white, a wondrous thrill.
Stars above in their diamond dress,
Whisper dreams in a gentle caress.

Ice mirrors the heavens, pure and bright,
Caught in cosmic, velvety night.
With every glance, a wish we weave,
In the icy air, we dare believe.

Nature's beauty, framed in blue,
As starlight dances in the dew.
Moments frozen, never fade,
In the silence, memories are made.

Through frosted panes, we take it in,
The universe whispers, we begin.
In starlit dreams, our hopes entwine,
Under the vast expanse, we shine.

A world asleep, yet full of grace,
In the stillness, we find our place.
Stargazing through the ice, we sigh,
As the universe breathes a gentle goodbye.

The Quiet of Falling Feathers

In whispers soft, the feathers glide,
A dance of peace, where stillness bides.
They touch the ground with gentle grace,
In silence found, the heart's embrace.

The trees stand tall, a watchful guard,
While nature rests, emotions marred.
Each flake a note in winter's song,
Where tranquil dreams and thoughts belong.

Beneath the sky, a silver hue,
The world transformed, both fresh and new.
In falling light, a calm reprieve,
A breath of hope for those who grieve.

The world slows down, a tender pause,
Each falling feather with no cause.
To feel the weight of what's untold,
A tale of warmth in the bitter cold.

In quietness, a message shared,
Of time to heal, of hearts laid bare.
So let the softest touches fall,
In feathered whispers, we find it all.

Night's Frozen Serenade

The moon casts shadows on the snow,
A silver path where soft winds blow.
Stars twinkle bright in the velvet deep,
While the world beneath begins to sleep.

Each breath is visible, a fleeting mist,
In frozen air, where dreams persist.
The silence hums a soothing tune,
Wrapped in the arms of a watchful moon.

Whispers carried on the chilled breeze,
As nature rests with effortless ease.
A serenade of night's embrace,
Transforms the dark with gentle grace.

Frost-kissed branches stand so still,
While shadows dance on the snowy hill.
The night unfolds its mystery,
A tranquil heart beats quietly.

In the stillness, time stands fast,
As echoes of the past are cast.
Each note a secret, fiercely bright,
In night's frozen serenade of light.

Hushed in Winter's Grasp

The world wrapped tight in white embrace,
Where shadows linger, time slows its pace.
Each flake a whisper, soft and round,
In winter's hold, a peace profound.

The pine trees hold their breath with care,
As crispness lingers in the air.
A blanket worn, the earth is still,
In hushed tones, we feel the chill.

Frosted windows frame the night,
While stars above shine fierce and bright.
A world serene, in silence clad,
As winter dreams of all we've had.

Footsteps crunch on paths they make,
Each sound a memory, soft to take.
In winter's hug, we find our way,
Held by the calm of a fading day.

We close our eyes and breathe it in,
The tranquil air like whispered sin.
In winter's grasp, we find our soul,
As night wraps us, making us whole.

Hidden Secrets in the Snow

Beneath the snow, the earth's heart beats,
In quiet corners where silence retreats.
Each flake a secret, held so tight,
Whispers of wonder veiled from sight.

Footprints lead to places unknown,
Where stories linger, seeds are sown.
A journey forged in winter's song,
In hidden truths, we all belong.

The chill reminds us of what's lost,
The warmth within, we count the cost.
Yet in the blanket, soft and white,
Lie hidden gems of pure delight.

Trees like sentinels guard the ways,
While shadows flicker in the haze.
Each breath a promise, softly shared,
In frozen realms, we are prepared.

So let us wander, hearts aglow,
In the endless fields of glistening snow.
For in each step, a secret grows,
A tapestry of hidden hopes.

Dances of the Icy Breeze

Whispers of winter kiss the trees,
The icy breeze begins to tease.
With every swirl, the snowflakes twirl,
Nature's ballet in a frozen whirl.

Chill in the air, crisp and light,
Dancing shadows, pure delight.
Footsteps soft on the powdered ground,
Joy in stillness, beauty is found.

Glistening frost on the window pane,
Each breath a cloud, a fleeting chain.
Nature's cadence, a gentle embrace,
In the hush of winter's grace.

From dawn till dusk, a sparkling scene,
Paths of white, so fresh and clean.
Moments linger, lost in time,
In the heart, a joyful rhyme.

Every flake, unique and rare,
Crafting wonders with tender care.
Under the dome of a pale blue sky,
The icy breeze sings lullabies.

The Frosted Dreamscape

A blanket white covers the ground,
In quiet whispers, dreams abound.
Frosted edges, a shimmering light,
Painting the world in pure delight.

Distant mountains, cloaked in white,
Silhouettes dance in the soft moonlight.
Every breath a shimmering cloud,
In this dreamland, warm and proud.

Trees adorned with crystals bright,
Sparkling jewels in the still of night.
Nature's canvas, vast and wide,
Filled with wonders, we cannot hide.

Stars twinkle like diamonds above,
Filling the night with warmth and love.
In this frost, our hearts align,
In the magical dreamscape, divine.

As dawn awakens, colors ignite,
The frosted world, a breathtaking sight.
In every heartbeat, joy will flow,
In this wondrous, frosty glow.

Beneath the Silver Stars

The night is draped in a velvet cloak,
Beneath the silver stars, we stoke.
Whispers of dreams float on the breeze,
In the quiet night, the heart finds ease.

Crickets sing their midnight tune,
A lullaby beneath the moon.
Shadows dance on the forest floor,
Each moment rich, a treasured lore.

Cool air wraps us in its embrace,
Under the stars, we find our place.
Glistening patterns that softly gleam,
In the deepness, we share our dream.

The world sleeps on, lost in the night,
While we gaze up at the glowing light.
In their brilliance, we find a spark,
Illuminating love in the dark.

With each heartbeat, the cosmos calls,
In this expanse, our spirit sprawls.
Beneath the stars, together we'll stay,
In the silence, our worries drift away.

Cold Embrace of Idleness

In winter's stillness, time stands still,
Wrapped in the cold, a moment to fill.
The world is hushed, the pace is slow,
In idle moments, thoughts begin to flow.

Frosty windows, a view so clear,
The calm of nature, drawing near.
Hot cocoa warms our hands on high,
In this serene space, we find the sky.

Snowflakes drift in a lazy dance,
A hush of beauty, a fleeting glance.
The hour stretches, calm and wide,
In idle hours, our dreams abide.

Outside, the world is wrapped in gray,
Yet in our hearts, the colors play.
In the cold embrace, we find our peace,
From the fast-paced life, we seek release.

So let us linger, let time unwind,
In the frost, peace we'll find.
In this idle moment, breathless and free,
The heart finds warmth, just you and me.

Memorable Mornings After White Nights

In the glow of dawn's embrace,
Memories linger, soft as lace.
Whispers of laughter, shadows play,
In gentle hues, the night fades away.

Coffee brews, a fragrant start,
Warmth wraps around each heart.
Soft sunlight spills on sleepy eyes,
Blankets of dreams, where comfort lies.

Echoes of stories shared and told,
Adventures sparked, courage bold.
With every sip, the past returns,
In morning light, a fire burns.

Birds take flight, a joyous song,
In this moment, we all belong.
The world awakens, fresh and bright,
Memorable mornings, pure delight.

The Beauty of Icy Stillness

Silent scenes of winter's grace,
Blankets glisten, still embrace.
Crystal branches, nature's art,
Frozen whispers touch the heart.

Reflecting pools of frozen glass,
Moments held, as hours pass.
In this calm, the world stands still,
Each breath a crisp and perfect thrill.

Footsteps echo in soft snow,
Through the woods, where cold winds blow.
Beneath the frost, life quietly waits,
As beauty shimmers, love radiates.

Stars above in velvet skies,
Glistening dreams, where silence lies.
The beauty of icy stillness reigns,
A peaceful heart, where joy remains.

Crystal Stars Above

In the night, a diamond sea,
Crystal stars, wild and free.
Whispers of wishes, softly bind,
Each twinkle a treasure, gently aligned.

Moonlight bathes the earth in glow,
Secrets shared with every flow.
Boundless beauty, a cosmic dance,
In the silence, all hearts prance.

Guiding hopes on velvet air,
Boundless dreams, beyond compare.
Stars remind us of our place,
In this vast, enchanting space.

Every flicker tells a tale,
Through darkness, love shall prevail.
Crystal stars, we gaze in awe,
Inspired by the wonder we saw.

Veils of Glimmering Frost

Morning breaks with frosty breath,
Veils of glimmering, nature's death.
Each blade of grass, a jewel's glow,
Winter's whisper, soft and slow.

Frozen patterns weave and curl,
In this spell, the cold winds whirl.
Delicate lace on branches cling,
Silent magic, winter's ring.

Beneath the frost, the world sleeps tight,
In crystal gowns, dressed in white.
Time stands still, a breathless trance,
In icy realms, our hearts advance.

Nature's canvas, pure and bright,
Veils of glimmering frost ignite.
With every dawn, each morning light,
We find our joy in winter's might.

Lonesome Flakes

Falling softly from the sky,
Each flake whispers all goodbye.
In the quiet, they dance low,
Marking paths where no one go.

Empty streets, the world is still,
Blanketed by winter's chill.
Echoes linger in the air,
A silent song, a frozen prayer.

Alone we wander, hearts so bare,
Lost in dreams of what we share.
Flakes like memories drift and fall,
Painting stories on winter's wall.

The night draws in, the shadows play,
Lonesome flakes take hearts away.
In their flight, a gentle grace,
Bringing peace to this cold space.

With each touch, they softly glow,
In their warmth, we come to know.
Even in solitude's embrace,
We find love in winter's face.

Tranquil Landscapes

Mountains rise in dawn's first light,
Painting skies with colors bright.
Rivers sing to tender trees,
Carrying whispers on the breeze.

Fields of gold and emerald green,
Nature's canvas, pure and clean.
Birds in flight, a graceful dance,
In each moment, a second chance.

Sunsets blaze with fiery hue,
While stars twinkle, fresh and new.
In this calm, our souls take flight,
In tranquil landscapes, pure delight.

Softly rests the evening's shade,
Where memories and dreams are made.
The heart finds peace, the spirit thrives,
In these lands, where nature lives.

Breathe in deep, feel life abound,
In every sight, in every sound.
This tranquil place, forever ours,
A sanctuary beneath the stars.

Echoes of the Flurries

Whispers dance in the cool of night,
Flurries swirl, a glistening sight.
Each soft touch, a fleeting kiss,
Echoes linger, pure bliss.

Footsteps crunch on frozen ground,
In silence, peace is found.
Ghostly forms in endless white,
Painting dreams in winter's light.

Time slows down in soft embrace,
Chasing shadows, finding grace.
Echoes hum a gentle tune,
Beneath the watchful, silver moon.

Snowflakes drift from skies above,
Wrapping all in endless love.
In this world, we lose our cares,
Journeying to where hope dares.

Whirling winds whisper our fate,
In the flurries, we await.
Echoes pause, a moment shared,
In this magic, hearts bared.

Under the Frosted Canopy

Beneath the boughs of frosted trees,
Nature whispers in the breeze.
Softly laid, a blanket white,
Cradling dreams in winter's night.

Shadows play in hidden nooks,
While time waits in quiet books.
Each branch dressed in icy lace,
A world transformed, a sacred space.

Hope ignites with every chill,
In this stillness, hearts we fill.
Underneath the stars' bright glow,
Life's beauty starts to gently show.

Snowflakes linger, holding grace,
A spark of warmth in this cold place.
Each breath taken beneath the sky,
A promise that we cannot deny.

Footprints lead through silver layers,
Tracing paths of hidden prayers.
Under the canopy, we roam,
Finding comfort, making home.

Solitude Under Stars

Beneath the vast and silent sky,
I find a peace that seldom sighs.
The stars above, they softly gleam,
In solitude, I dare to dream.

The moonlight whispers tales untold,
Of dreams once bright and hearts of gold.
In quietude, my thoughts take flight,
A canvas painted with the night.

Each twinkle beckons, secrets share,
In this embrace, I shed my care.
The gentle breeze sings lullabies,
While solitude beneath stars lies.

The universe, a vast array,
Reminds me of my heart's ballet.
With every spark, I feel the ties,
That bind my soul to starry skies.

So here I dwell, in peaceful thought,
Embraced by dreams that time forgot.
In solitude, I find my art,
A universe within my heart.

Snowflakes in the Dark

Falling softly through the night,
Whispers dance in chilly light.
Snowflakes twirl like fleeting dreams,
Silent nights unveil their themes.

Each flake, unique in fragile grace,
Gently lands in a timeless place.
In the dark, their beauty glows,
A serenity that nature bestows.

The world is wrapped in a quilted white,
Magic lingers, pure delight.
Underneath the velvet sky,
Snowflakes mingle, softly sigh.

Footsteps crunch on frosty ground,
In this stillness, peace is found.
Nature's breath, a crisp embrace,
In the dark, we find our space.

As they fall, old worries fade,
In their presence, joy is laid.
Snowflakes in the dark conspire,
To inspire dreams that lift us higher.

Cold Embrace

In winter's grip, the world stands still,
A chilling breath, a sudden thrill.
Frosted air wraps like a shawl,
In cold embrace, I feel it all.

The trees wear coats of crystal white,
Underneath, the earth feels light.
Every shadow holds a tale,
Of whispered winds that start to wail.

Embers fade in the quiet dark,
While silence hums a tranquil spark.
Beneath the frost, life stirs awake,
In this cold embrace, hearts do break.

Magic swirls in frigid air,
Inviting dreams beyond compare.
In the stillness, we find our grace,
Within the confines of cold embrace.

So hold me close, sweet winter night,
Together we embrace the light.
For in this chill, we find the fire,
That warms our souls and lifts us higher.

Ethereal Stillness

In twilight's glow, the world stands bare,
A breath of peace hangs in the air.
Ethereal stillness wraps the night,
My heart dances in gentle flight.

Shadows stretch, the moon ascends,
A moment where the silence bends.
In this hush, the stars awake,
As dreams are woven, hearts partake.

With every pause, the world unfolds,
Stories whispered, secrets told.
Time holds still, a fleeting glance,
In twilight's dance, we find our chance.

The night's embrace, a calming balm,
In stillness, find my heartbeat's calm.
Ethereal light, a kiss so soft,
Guides me gently, lifts me aloft.

Amidst the quiet, I lose my place,
In this stillness, I find grace.
Ethereal whispers call my name,
In the night where stars became.

Frosty Mornings Awakened

Chill in the air, a breath so clear,
Trees stand silent, their branches drear.
Sunlight peeks through the frosty veil,
Morning whispers a magical tale.

Footsteps crunch on the sparkling ground,
Each sound dances, a joyous sound.
Birds awaken with a gentle song,
In this moment, the world feels strong.

Steam rises from mugs held tight,
Warmth embraced in the soft daylight.
Noses tingle, cheeks are red,
Dreams unfurl where the memories tread.

A world transformed with crystal light,
Nature's canvas, pure and bright.
Every corner, a sight so grand,
Frosty mornings, a wonderland.

Winter's Quiet Wish

In the stillness, a hush prevails,
Snowflakes drift like whispering trails.
Blankets of white on the earth so deep,
Winter's dreams in silence keep.

Fireplace crackles, stories unfold,
Hearts grow warm as the night turns cold.
Outside, the world in soft repose,
A tranquil peace that gently flows.

Stars twinkle bright in the evening sky,
Silent wishes as the night drifts by.
Moonlight dances on frosted boughs,
Nature rests and takes its vows.

Footprints left in the powdery snow,
Each step tells where the heart must go.
In the stillness, dreams intertwine,
Winter's wish, a moment divine.

Dance of the Falling Flakes

Twirl and swirl in the winter's breeze,
Flakes descend with such graceful ease.
Each one unique, a masterpiece,
Nature's ballet, a soft release.

Children laughing, their joy takes flight,
Snowmen rise in the fading light.
Snowballs tossed in a playful spree,
Winter's magic, wild and free.

Branches dressed in a glistening coat,
Each flake whispers, each flake floats.
Underneath skies of pastel gray,
The dance continues throughout the day.

As dusk approaches, colors ignite,
Creating a canvas, a wondrous sight.
In the silence, we hear the song,
Of falling flakes where dreams belong.

Twilight in the Snow

Shadows lengthen as daylight fades,
Twilight settles, a soft cascade.
Colors shift in the cool night air,
Whispers of magic linger there.

Snowflakes shimmer like diamonds rare,
Reflecting glimmers, the world laid bare.
Footprints vanish, the past erased,
In twilight's glow, a moment embraced.

The quiet speaks, a serenade,
Holding secrets in the day's parade.
Stars emerge, one by one, they glow,
A tapestry woven in twilight's flow.

Underneath the vast expanse,
Nature's beauty offers a chance.
To pause, reflect, and simply be,
In twilight's embrace, we feel so free.

Echoes in Crystal

Whispers float on winter's breath,
Promises made in the silent depth.
Footsteps crunch on icy ground,
Heartbeats echo, softly found.

Crystal dreams in frosty air,
Stars above in a silver glare.
Memories wrapped in fragile light,
Dancing shadows in the night.

Branches draped in frozen lace,
A stillness time cannot erase.
Each twinkle tells a timeless tale,
As spirits wander, bright and pale.

Moonlight spills like molten glass,
Through the trees, where secrets pass.
Nature's symphony, soft and clear,
Echoes whisper, drawing near.

Embers fade, the moment's sway,
Crystal echoes fade away.
Yet in silence, spirits sing,
In our hearts, they take to wing.

A Tapestry of White

Snowflakes fall, a gentle sigh,
Blanketing the world up high.
Each flake unique, a fleeting art,
Weaving dreams that warm the heart.

Fields of white stretch far and wide,
Underneath the winter's tide.
Footprints trace a winding line,
Stories told where shadows twine.

Evergreens dressed in frosty crowns,
Nature's splendor all around.
Whispers float on chilly gusts,
In this wonder, pure and just.

Icicles hang, sharp and clear,
Glistening like a precious tear.
Sunlight sparkles on the scene,
A tapestry, soft and serene.

Quiet moments, breathless pause,
In this beauty, endless cause.
Wrapped in white, the world stands still,
In winter's grasp, hearts softly thrill.

Frost-Kissed Reveries

Morning breaks with silver light,
Frosty breath, a pure delight.
Lace on windows, nature's art,
Whispers linger, softly start.

Each step cracks the frozen floor,
Echoing dreams of days before.
In the chill, the heart feels warm,
Wrapped in snow, a gentle charm.

Chirps of birds through branches sweet,
Nature's chorus, purest feat.
Beneath the frost, life stirs anew,
Awakening when skies turn blue.

Crisp and clear, the world awaits,
Frost-kissed dreams, opening gates.
Inhale the wonder, exhale the woes,
Feasting on the magic that winter shows.

Frozen rivers, glistening flow,
Carrying tales from long ago.
In the stillness, whispers play,
Frost-kissed reveries lead the way.

Starlit Chill

In the night, the starlight glows,
Whispers curl where the night wind blows.
Moonbeams dance on velvet skies,
Casting spells, a soft disguise.

Each twinkle holds a secret dream,
Rippling light on a silver stream.
In the chill, the world slows down,
Wrapped in shadows, nature's gown.

Crisp the air, a haunting song,
Echoes linger, soft and strong.
Underneath the cosmic whirl,
Hearts entwined in a gentle swirl.

Frosty breath in the quiet night,
Every star, a beacon bright.
Paths of wonder carved in peace,
In this stillness, troubles cease.

Chilled by night, but warmed by light,
Dreams take flight in the soft twilight.
Starlit moments, ever dear,
In winter's hold, we persevere.

Midnight in the Chill

Whispers in the icy air,
Moonlight dancing with despair.
Shadows stretch across the ground,
Silence hangs without a sound.

Stars above like diamonds shine,
Night wraps all in velvet twine.
In the stillness, dreams take flight,
Midnight's chill brings sweet delight.

Snowflakes fall, a gentle grace,
Blanketing the earth's cold face.
Breath of winter, crisp and bright,
Sparks of warmth in frozen night.

Far away, a distant toll,
Time moves slow, it tugs the soul.
Every heartbeat like a drum,
In this night, we all become.

Hidden paths through frosty trees,
Rustling leaves in whispered breeze.
Nature's hush, an old refrain,
Midnight's chill, our hearts remain.

Glimmering Haze

Morning breaks with colors grand,
Glimmers dance across the land.
Mist ascends, a soft embrace,
Nature's beauty, slow-paced grace.

Glistening fields with dew-kissed cheer,
Promise of warmth as day draws near.
Sunburst beams through foggy veil,
Painting dreams where hopes set sail.

Winds whisper sweet secrets anew,
Every moment feels so true.
A tapestry of light and shade,
In this haze, memories fade.

Birdsongs lift the heart to fly,
As the world begins to sigh.
Glimmering trails in morning light,
Breathe in deep, the world feels right.

Let this joy weave through your heart,
In the glow of light, we start.
Glimmering haze, so pure and bright,
Filling souls with warmth and light.

Starlit Frost

In the quiet of the night,
Stars amaze with twinkling light.
Frosty air around me sways,
Painting dreams in silver haze.

Whispers echo through the dark,
Nature sings its frozen spark.
Each soft flake, a work of art,
Cold and still, it warms the heart.

Moonlit paths invite my gaze,
Through the night, my spirit plays.
Starlit frost on every tree,
A serene world, pure and free.

Crystals dance in frosty air,
Every breath, a whispered prayer.
In the stillness, magic grows,
Underneath the starlit glows.

Time stands still in this embrace,
Frosted air, a gentle place.
With each step, my soul takes flight,
Lost in wonder, through the night.

Enchanted Winter's Breath

The world adorned in white so fair,
Whispers dance on frosty air.
Winter's breath, a soft caress,
Nature's magic in its dress.

Boughs are heavy, draped in snow,
Silent beauty, all aglow.
Footprints carved in crystal sheen,
Echo of where we have been.

Flakes descend like fleeting dreams,
Glistening in the sun's warm beams.
Every flake unique, divine,
In this moment, time aligns.

Candles flicker, fires glow,
Hearts are warm amidst the snow.
In the hush, our spirits soar,
Enchanted breath forevermore.

Gather close and share a tale,
Through the night, let love prevail.
Winter's breath, a gentle song,
In this magic, we belong.

Frosted Whispers

In the stillness of the night,
Whispers dance on icy air,
Each flake a fleeting song,
Softly weaving through the bare.

Moonlight kisses snowy ground,
Creating magic, pure and bright,
The world in silence wrapped,
Cradled close in gentle light.

Branches bow with heavy grace,
Shimmering in frosted sheen,
Nature's breath is soft and slow,
In this calm, we're all serene.

Footsteps crunch on frozen crust,
Echoes of the winter's muse,
Every sound a tender hush,
In this frost, we softly choose.

Time stands still, a quiet plea,
Within the fragile, glistening,
Frosted whispers softly fade,
As dawn begins its awakening.

Hushed in White

A blanket stretches, pure and wide,
Covering the earth in white,
Softly muffled, the world sighs,
As day turns gently into night.

Footfalls quiet on the snow,
Breath like steam, a fleeting sign,
Muted colors, shadows blend,
In this moment, all is fine.

Icicles hang like crystal tears,
Adorning rooftops, evergreen,
Nature holds her breath in dreams,
Hushed in white, a tranquil scene.

Winter's grasp, both bold and meek,
Every branch a work of art,
Silent whispers fill the air,
Touching gently, heart to heart.

In the cool embrace of night,
Stars twinkle in a frosty glaze,
Hushed in white, we find our peace,
Lost in winter's gentle ways.

Icicles and Shadows

Icicles dangle, sharp and true,
Casting shadows on soft white,
Nature's art, so bold and bare,
In the heart of frosted night.

Whispers travel on the breeze,
Stories wrapped in chilly air,
Each breath like smoke, a memory,
In this world, we share a care.

Moonlight throws its silver glow,
Painting paths on frozen ground,
Each corner hides a secret glimpse,
In the hush, no voice is found.

Underneath the pale moon's watch,
Stars collide, a cosmic dance,
In the silence, shadows creep,
Nature slips into a trance.

Time drips slow, like melting frost,
Moments hang, in still repose,
Icicles sparkle as they fall,
Touching hearts where winter goes.

Crystal Silence

In the night there lies a peace,
Crystal silence fills the void,
Every sound seems far away,
All distractions now destroyed.

Frost adorns the windowpanes,
Each design a fleeting dream,
Nature's brush strokes paint the air,
Like a gentle, silver stream.

Beneath the stars, a world anew,
Wrapped in stillness, soft and whole,
Footsteps whisper on the ground,
Echoes of the wandering soul.

Trees stand tall, a secret guard,
Holding stories yet untold,
In the quiet, hearts confide,
Cloaked in winter's tender cold.

As dawn approaches, hush remains,
In this crystal, silent grace,
We find solace in the glow,
Of a world, our hearts embrace.

Dreams Beneath the Drift

Whispers of snowflakes fall,
Painting tales upon the ground.
Stars reflect in frozen dreams,
As time drifts softly around.

Beneath the silent, pale light,
Memories whisper, softly swirl.
In the cloak of winter's night,
Dreams awaken, softly twirl.

Footsteps crunch in crystal air,
Echoes dance in frosty breeze.
In the stillness, hearts lay bare,
Trusting fate will grant them ease.

Glistening in moonlit grace,
Winter weaves her tender quilt.
Beneath the drift, we embrace,
A world anew, yet softly built.

As dawn breaks, shadows recede,
Hope unfurls like wings in flight.
In the dreams that winter seed,
Life awakens, pure and bright.

Winter's Lullaby

Softly falls the white embrace,
Tucking earth in slumber deep.
Nature hums a tender tune,
As the world begins to sleep.

Frosty breath on window panes,
Drawing pictures, wild and free.
In this hush, life gently wanes,
Winter sings its melody.

Blankets spread o'er hill and tree,
Covering all that was and is.
In the cold, a sign of glee,
Hearts ignited with winter's bliss.

Footsteps linger, echo clear,
As the night draws close and wide.
In the silence, whispers near,
Winter's song, a tender guide.

Dreams float softly in the air,
Cradled by the moon's soft glow.
In this world, devoid of care,
Feel the peace of winter's flow.

Veils of December

Veils of white, so soft, so pure,
Shroud the earth in whispered grace.
Every moment we endure,
Wrapped in winter's warm embrace.

Crimson leaves now pass away,
Bowing low, they kiss the ground.
In the chill, we find our way,
Silent echoes, love profound.

Frosted branches, trees adorned,
Nature's art in stark display.
In this quiet, hearts are warmed,
Stolen treasures, come what may.

Glimmers dance on frozen streams,
Reflecting worlds we cannot see.
In the night, we chase our dreams,
Hidden paths, forever free.

With each breath, the coldest air,
Fills our lungs with dreams unspoken.
In December's tender care,
Find the bond that won't be broken.

Frozen Serenade

In the stillness, shadows play,
Stars like whispers in the night.
Frosty winds begin to sway,
While the world holds its breath tight.

Moonlight drapes the vale in silk,
Waking echoes of the past.
Every flake a drop of milk,
Nurturing dreams meant to last.

Trees adorned in icy lace,
Nature's jewels, shimmering bright.
In this transient, tender space,
Hearts find comfort in the light.

Songs of winter, soft and clear,
Carried on the chilly breeze.
In the quiet, all is near,
Moments cherished, hearts at ease.

As tomorrow breaks anew,
Frost will lift and light will play.
In the beauty, dreams come true,
In the warmth of a brand new day.

Remnants of a Chilling Whirlwind

Whispers dance through barren trees,
Ghosts of autumn in the breeze.
Leaves that crumble, crisp and light,
Echoes fade into the night.

Silent paths where shadows creep,
Memories in the silence seep.
Nature's breath, a whispered song,
In the chill where echoes throng.

Clouds that mirror icy thoughts,
Blanket dreams that time forgot.
In the void where warmth retreats,
Coldness wraps in winding sheets.

Footsteps crunch on frozen ground,
Every move a solemn sound.
Underneath the waning light,
Secrets shiver in the night.

Fractured skies, a hint of gray,
As the daylight fades away.
Remnants dance like fleeting sighs,
In the winds that haunt the skies.

Veils of Frosty Twilight

In the hush of evening's veil,
Frosty whispers start to trail.
Stars awake with glimmer bright,
Casting dreams in soft twilight.

Shadows stretch on frozen ground,
Nature's heartbeat, a quiet sound.
Veils of mist, a ghostly throng,
Bathed in hues of dusk's sweet song.

Branches drape with crystal lace,
Artistry of time and space.
Every breath a cloud of white,
Hanging softly in the night.

Echoes of the day depart,
Leaving echoes in the heart.
Whispers linger, soft and clear,
Blooming dreams draw ever near.

In the twilight's frosty grip,
Life finds beauty in the slip.
Veils enfold the world in light,
As the day gives way to night.

Radiance in the Chill of Night

Moonlight bathes the world in grace,
Radiance in a cooling space.
Stars like diamonds scatter wide,
Guiding dreams on silver tide.

Whispers weave through shadowed lanes,
Carried soft on icy stains.
In the chill, a spark ignites,
Filling hearts with quiet delights.

Frosted breath in midnight's glow,
Painting tales of ebb and flow.
Every glimmer speaks of bright,
Hopeful hues in the chill of night.

Silent beats of time unspooled,
In this realm where magic ruled.
Night's embrace, a tender sigh,
Lifts the spirits, sets them high.

Radiance beams from winter's heart,
Crafting beauty, a work of art.
In the stillness, warmth can thrive,
Illuminating souls alive.

The Eldritch Silence

In the depths where shadows dwell,
Listen close, a secret spell.
Eldritch whispers fill the air,
Echoes of forgotten care.

Time stands still, suspended breath,
Chilling whispers speak of death.
Yet within this eerie space,
Lies a beauty, dark and grace.

Moonlit paths twist and unwind,
Every corner, a tale confined.
In silence, mysteries arise,
Glimmers hidden from the eyes.

Darkness wraps with gentle hands,
Holding close what understanding lands.
In each pause, a world takes flight,
Finding joy in endless night.

Eldritch silence breathes with might,
A tender dance of dark and light.
In the stillness, truth resides,
Where the unseen often hides.

Tranquility in a Frozen World

In silence deep, the snowflakes fall,
A blanket white, encompassing all.
Whispers of frost in the chilly air,
Nature's peace, a gentle prayer.

Time stretches long, as shadows bend,
The icy landscape knows no end.
Stars twinkle bright in the velvet night,
A tranquil hush, a soothing sight.

Footprints left in the morning light,
A story told, pure and white.
Frozen breath escapes in clouds,
While winter weaves its crystal shrouds.

Branches bowed with glistening weight,
All life rests, a moment to wait.
In stillness found within the chill,
Echoes of joy, a heart to fill.

Embraced by the silver glow,
Time slows down in the afterglow.
Tranquility reigns, a sacred space,
In this frozen world, I find my place.

Midnight's Frigid Waltz

Under the moon's soft, watchful eye,
Whispers of winter drift and sigh.
The world adorned in sparkling white,
As shadows dance in the pale moonlight.

A chill in the air, crisp and clear,
Midnight's waltz draws near and near.
Stars twirl above in a cosmic trance,
While snowflakes sway in a graceful dance.

Branches sway in the cold night breeze,
Frozen moments, a heart to seize.
Each flake a story, a fleeting thought,
In this stillness, peace is sought.

Footfalls echo on the frozen ground,
A melody plays without a sound.
The world slows its hurried pace,
Caught in the beauty, a warm embrace.

With every breath, a frosty plume,
Night wraps us in its silent gloom.
Under the stars, we find our bliss,
In midnight's waltz, a perfect kiss.

Flickering Hopes in the Snow

Amidst the blizzard, dreams arise,
Flickers of hope beneath gray skies.
Softly they glow like distant stars,
Guiding us through the winter's scars.

Each flake a promise, fresh and new,
Cloaked in wonder, a vibrant hue.
In the silence, hearts ignite,
A dance of warmth in the cold of night.

Snow-covered paths lead us forth,
To seek the beauty held in worth.
In every drift, a tale unfolds,
Of flickering hopes and dreams of gold.

With laughter echoing in the freeze,
We chase the light with effortless ease.
In each falling flake, we see our fate,
Unfolding gently, never too late.

A spark within, to guide us on,
Through frosty nights until the dawn.
Flickering hopes, forever will grow,
In the heart of winter, love will flow.

Enigma of the Frozen Hour

In twilight's embrace, shadows blend,
The frozen hour begins to descend.
Mysteries linger in the evening air,
As nature holds her secrets rare.

Frozen leaves whisper tales untold,
In the twilight's grip, both fierce and cold.
The clock ticks softly, in rhythm slow,
An enigma wrapped in winter's glow.

Crystals glitter on branches bare,
Each sparkling shard a fleeting stare.
Time dances lightly on frost-coated ground,
In the frozen hour, calm is found.

Silence deepens, the world holds its breath,
In this moment, we dance with death.
Yet hope glimmers in the dark's embrace,
A soft reminder of love's sweet grace.

As stars emerge in the cold abyss,
The frozen hour, a moment of bliss.
In the heart of winter, we come alive,
For in these shadows, our dreams shall thrive.

Whispers of Frost

In the quiet of the night,
Whispers of frost take flight.
Stars twinkle with icy grace,
Nature wears a gentle lace.

Trees stand tall, cloaked in white,
Silent echoes in soft light.
Moonlight dances on the ground,
Magic in the stillness found.

A breath of chill fills the air,
While shadows play without a care.
Footsteps crunch on frozen dew,
The world a canvas dipped in blue.

Every flake a story told,
In the arms of winter's fold.
Time slows down, a perfect pause,
In the beauty winter draws.

As dawn breaks with golden hue,
Whispers fade, but dreams renew.
With every sunrise, hope is cast,
In the warmth that comes at last.

Shimmering Silence

In the stillness of the night,
Snowflakes fall, a pure delight.
Each one glimmers in the light,
A shimmering silent sight.

Winds embrace the frozen trees,
Whispering through the icy breeze.
Silent dreams in soft repose,
Nature's song, a gentle prose.

Footprints lead to worlds unknown,
Where winter's magic has been sown.
In soft blankets, earth is swayed,
By shimmering silence, gently laid.

Stars above, like diamonds gleam,
Celestial whispers, a shared dream.
In the quiet, hearts ignite,
Finding peace in endless night.

As the world holds its breath tight,
In the cradle of soft light.
Hope emerges, bright and bold,
In the tales of winter told.

Winter's Veil

Winter's veil drapes soft and slow,
Covering earth in a gentle glow.
Every branch and meadow fair,
Wrapped in beauty, beyond compare.

Whispers linger on the breeze,
Telling tales of ancient trees.
A canvas white, serene and wide,
Where secrets and shadows quietly hide.

Frosty breath upon the pane,
In this realm, no room for pain.
Life slows down, the world takes pause,
In the magic that winter draws.

Time feels still beneath the stars,
As night reveals its frozen scars.
Twinkling lights in the distance gleam,
Guiding us through a frosty dream.

With every flake that gently falls,
A symphony of nature calls.
In winter's embrace, pure and true,
We find solace, and courage too.

Midnight in the Winter Realm

At midnight, shadows start to play,
In winter's realm where cold holds sway.
The world is silent, blanketed white,
A tranquil hush, a cozy sight.

Stars shimmer like frost on the ground,
In the stillness, a heartbeat sound.
Whispers dance through the frosty air,
Where dreams unfold without a care.

The moonlight casts a silver hue,
Painting paths where lovers drew.
Every breath a cloud of sighs,
In the magic where silence lies.

Crystals sparkle, the night so bright,
In the embrace of winter's light.
A world reborn, pure and bold,
In these midnight stories told.

With every heartbeat, life renews,
In the depth of snowy views.
A serene journey waits to start,
In winter's arms, we find our heart.

Milton Keynes UK
Ingram Content Group UK Ltd.
UKHW010228111224
452348UK00011B/581

9 789916 794753